PROVERBS

UNCOMMON SENSE

Connect with God. Connect with Others.
Connect with Life.

Proverbs: Uncommon Sense
Youth Edition Student Book
© 2006 Serendipity
Reprinted January 2007, June 2007, June 2008

Published by LifeWay Press®
Nashville, Tennessee

ISBN: 1-5749-4284-0
Item Number: 001303838

Dewey Decimal Classification: 223.7
Subject Headings:
BIBLE O.T. PROVERBS—STUDY \ CHRISTIAN LIFE

Printed in the United States of America

Student Ministry Publishing
LifeWay Church Resources
One LifeWay Plaza
Nashville, TN   37234-0174

We believe that the Bible has God for its author; salvation for its end; and truth, without any mixture of error, for its matter and that all Scripture is totally true and trustworthy. The 2000 statement of *The Baptist Faith and Message* is our doctrinal guideline.

13 12 11 10 09 08 07   2 3 4 5 6 7 8 9 10

CONTENTS

EXPERIENCE

Combine *teaching that engages a large-group* with dynamic *small-group experiences and discussions* and you end up grappling with reality and experiencing real life change. Throughout 13 sessions, small groups will find power in just being together and connecting.

 Get Ready

To get the most from this experience, spend some time with God each day leading up to your group session. Wrap your brain around the short Bible passages, listen to God, and jot down thoughts and insights.

 LifePoint

Your large-group leader will welcome everyone. You'll hear the "LifePoint" or big idea for the session, and then divide into small groups.

 Say What?

Enjoy fun, interactive experiences and discussions in your small group. Discuss the "Random Question of the Week" and join activities or discussions that lead into the session topic.

 So What?

The master-teacher will lead the entire group in understanding what God has to say on the topic. Content is deep, but engaging. Follow along, jot notes, and respond to questions in your book.

 Do What?

All study should direct us toward action and life change. It's easier and more helpful to discuss application in small groups. The goal is to be real with each other in order to connect with God and each other. Find power in the support and prayers of other students.

 Now What?

To see real power in your life, you don't want to leave the session and just go on with life as normal. The "Now What?" assignments help you continue your journey and give you an opportunity to go deeper with God.

AT A GLANCE

Get Ready

Daily time with God
& your journal

LifePoint

Large Group:
Welcome & Theme

Say What?

Small Group:
Fun & Interaction

So What?

Large Group:
Teaching & Discovery
(Master Teacher)

Do What?

Small Group:
Getting Real
& Connecting

now What?

Continue your journey...

GROUP COVENANT

It is important that your group covenant together, agreeing to live out important group values. Once these values are agreed upon, your group will be on its way to experiencing true Christian community. It's very important that your group discuss these values—preferably as you begin this study. The first session would be most appropriate. (Check the rules to which each member of your group agrees.)

☐ Priority: While you are in this course of study, you give the group meetings priority.

☐ Participation: Everyone is encouraged to participate and no one dominates.

☐ Respect: Everyone is given the right to his or her own opinion, and all questions are encouraged and respected.

☐ Confidentiality: Anything that is said in the meeting is never repeated outside the meeting without permission. *Note: Church staff may be required by law to report illegal activities.*

☐ Life Change: We will regularly assess our own progress in applying *LifePoints* and encourage one another in our pursuit of becoming more like Christ.

☐ Care and Support: Permission is given to call upon each other at any time, especially in times of crisis. The group will provide care for every member.

☐ Accountability: We agree to let the members of the group hold us accountable to the commitments we make in whatever loving ways we decide upon. Unsolicited advice giving is not permitted.

☐ Empty Chair: The group is open to welcoming new people at every meeting.

☐ Mission: We agree as a group to reach out and invite others to join us.

☐ Ministry: We will encourage one another to volunteer and serve in a ministry and to support missions by giving financially and/or personally serving.

WISDOM: LEARNIG TO LIVE LIFE WITH SKILL

 Get Ready

Read one of these short Bible passages each day, and spend a few minutes wrapping your brain around it. Be sure to jot down any insights you discover.

MONDAY

Read Proverbs 1:1-6

How would you define wisdom? Why is wisdom important in the life of a follower of Christ?

TUESDAY

Read Proverbs 1:7; 9:10-12

Have you ever made unwise choices? What would you say were the results of your unwise choices? How have unwise choices affected you spiritually?

WEDNESDAY

Read Proverbs 2:1-5

What is something you practice doing? Why do you spend time practicing? How can you spend time searching for wisdom? Why should you search for wisdom?

THURSDAY **Read Proverbs 3:5-6**

What does it mean to "Trust in the Lord"? Have you ever been tempted to follow wisdom from someone other than God?

FRIDAY **Read Proverbs 3:7-8**

What is the difference between having wisdom in your own eyes and having wisdom in God's eyes? Which is better? Why?

SATURDAY **Read Proverbs 3:25-26**

What figurative snares, traps, have caught you? What snares in life have you been able to avoid? Was it easier to be trapped or to avoid being trapped? Explain.

SUNDAY **Read Matthew 7:24-27**

What is the difference between a house that is built on the rock and a house that is built on the sand? Spiritually, how can you learn the difference between a "rock" and "sand"? Are you building your house on the rock or the sand?

 LifePoint

Wisdom is a skill that is learned throughout life. However, contrary to popular belief, wisdom does not refer to knowledge or intelligence.

**ALL-GROUP
TIME:**
Divide into
ler groups of
preferably in
rcle. You will
ave a small-
up leader for
"Say What?"

 # Say What? *(15 MINUTES)*

Random Question of the Week:
When was the last time you had a milk moustache?

Group Experience: Puzzling Questions
Work together to discover the answers to these puzzling questions:

1. Two sons and two fathers go fishing. They each catch one fish. The total number of fish they catch is three. How is this possible?

2. A man comes home one day and begins to check his e-mail when he discovers Myrtle lying on the floor, dead. There is broken glass and a large quantity of water on the floor. What happened?

3. You have two traditional hourglass timers. One is a seven-minute timer and the other is an eleven-minute timer. You want to boil an ostrich egg for exactly 15 minutes. How do you do it? How soon after the start of the whole process will the egg be ready?

After the exercise, answer these follow-up questions:

1. How did these questions make you feel?

2. Do you have to resist giving up when the questions are difficult?

3. How did you feel when you received advice that didn't help you answer the questions?

4. Finish this sentence: The best advice ever given to me was...

So What? *(25 MINUTES)*

A Wise Request

1. What is the definition of wisdom?

The ability to discern or judge what is true, right or lasting.

2. How did Solomon become wise?

He asked God for it.

Learning from the Bible

¹ The proverbs of Solomon son of David, king of Israel:

² For gaining wisdom and being instructed;

for understanding insightful sayings;

³ for receiving wise instruction

[in] righteousness, justice, and integrity;

⁴ for teaching shrewdness to the inexperienced, knowledge and discretion to a young man—

⁵ a wise man will listen and increase his learning, and a discerning man will obtain guidance—

⁶ for understanding a proverb or a parable, the words of the wise, and their riddles.

⁷ The fear of the LORD is the beginning of knowledge;

fools despise wisdom and instruction.

Proverbs 1:1-7

Learning to Live Life with Skill...WISDOM

3. For whom was the book of Proverbs written?

People

4. Most people don't know the difference between ___*intellegence*___ *knowledge* and ___*wisdom*___.

5. What is intelligence?

the ability to learn .

6. What is knowledge?

Facts you remember

7. From what two sources can we acquire wisdom?

- *School* ~~class~~ *observation*
- *bible* *from God*

8. What is one way that paying attention in life has made you wise?

~~staying~~ *Making notes during class*
Learn by ~~learning~~ your own

Learning the Value of Wisdom...

9. What are three actions that wise men do?

- *fear the LORD* - *discipline*
- *let wise listen*
- *let discerning get guidance*

Laying the Wisdom Foundation

10. On what is true wisdom based?

- *fear*
- *respect*

11. True wisdom is associated with ___ *God* ___ .

12. Why isn't the fear of the Lord an old-fashioned concept?

God judges.

11

Do What? *(20 MINUTES)*

Group Experience: Making It Personal

1. Does knowing King Solomon as the wisest man to ever live help you dig deeper into the Proverbs for wisdom? Why or why not?

2. How would you describe someone with a healthy fear of God?

3. Which area of your life causes you to struggle the most in regards to wisdom?
   - ☐ Learning from others' mistakes
   - ☒ Understanding and learning from my own mistakes
   - ☒ Spending time gaining knowledge from the Bible
   - ☐ Developing a healthy view of the "fear" of God
   - ☐ Not consciously trying to gain wisdom
   - ☐ Other:

4. Complete this sentence: In order to gain wisdom, I need to

-focus on God 1st
- Ask God for widsom
Pray for help.

Wisdom is a skill that is learned throughout life. However, contrary to popular belief, wisdom does not refer to knowledge or intelligence.

These "Do" Points will help you grab hold of this week's LifePoint. Be open and honest as you answer the questions within your small group.

1. <u>Commit to discover wise people.</u> You become like the people who surround you. This isn't just a cute saying; it's true! Have you ever thought about the way you talk? Do you have an accent? Where did you get your accent? You take on the characteristics of the people around you.
   Are you surrounding yourself with wise people who will encourage you to fill your life with wisdom?

2. <u>Search for wisdom in God's Word.</u> The Bible is full of proverbs that give us instructions about how we are to live our lives. We don't just read the Bible like we read a novel for our English class. The Bible sheds God's light onto our lives and reveals areas where we are in need of wisdom.
   Have you spent time searching God's Word for wisdom lately?

3. <u>Develop a healthy fear of the Lord.</u> As you develop wisdom in your life, you will continually have the option to live your life for yourself or for God.
   As you increase your wisdom, how can a healthy fear of the Lord be a positive thing?

Prayer Connection:

This is the time to encourage, support, and pray for each other in our journeys to grasp who God really is and how much He cares for each of us.

Share prayer needs with the group, especially those related to knowing and connecting with God. Your group facilitator will close your time in prayer.

Prayer Needs:

Remember your "Get Ready" daily Bible readings and questions at the beginning of Session 2.

 # now What?

Deepen your understanding of who God is, and continue the journey you've begun today by choosing one of the following assignments to complete this week:

Option #1:

If you enjoy writing, take the time this week to write down any wise actions that you notice. Spend time searching for wisdom. When you notice wisdom occurring around you, take the time to write down what you see. Be prepared to share your observations with your small group next week.

Option #2:

Take some time this week to re-write Proverbs 1:1-7 in your own words. Feel free to paraphrase the passage or rewrite it in paragraph form. The important thing is to grasp and communicate the meaning of the passage. Then find a photograph from a magazine or newspaper or even your favorite Web site that reminds you of this Scripture. Be prepared to share your thoughts with your small group next week.

Bible Reference Notes

Use these notes to deepen your understanding as you study the Bible on your own:

Proverbs 1:2

gaining wisdom. The main theme in Proverbs is wisdom, the nature of it and how to obtain it. The proverbs are common-sense guidelines for living. They teach that fearing the Lord is the beginning of wisdom (v. 7).

Proverbs 1:3

wise instruction. This is training in everyday actions, attitudes, and character that will lead to true success in life.

Proverbs 1:7

fear of the Lord. The fear of the Lord involves acknowledging God's power and sovereignty, then offering our obedience in light of it. The fool disregards God's presence and power, acting as if personal satisfaction is all that matters.

Proverbs 2:1-3

The writer repeatedly appeals to his son to live a life of wisdom.

Proverbs 2:4

seek ... treasure. This is an apt comparison. To find treasure one must search, dig, and excavate. Finding wisdom requires similar activity.

Proverbs 2:5

then you will understand. When we search for wisdom, we find God Himself, and our relationship with Him deepens.

Proverbs 3:5

with all your heart. The Bible uses this phrase to express total commitment. The "Shema" in Deuteronomy 6:5 calls us to love God with all our hearts, minds, and souls. Jesus described this as the first and greatest commandment.

Proverbs 3:6

guide ... paths. This implies more than guidance. It means God intentionally removes obstacles from our path.

NOTES

2

STICKS AND STONES AND...
WORDS: THEY ALL HURT

 Get Ready

Read one of these short Bible passages each day and spend a few minutes wrapping your brain around it. Be sure to jot down any insights you discover.

MONDAY

Read Proverbs 12:14; 13:3; 18:21
How important is your mouth? What makes your words so important to you? What "fruits" are coming from your mouth?

TUESDAY

Read Proverbs 18:2,13
How important is it to listen to others? Which is harder for you—to listen to other people's thoughts or to share your own? Why?

WEDNESDAY

Read Proverbs 18:8 *not sure*   *don't know*
What makes gossip so satisfying? Why do we gossip about others? How does spreading gossip about others make us feel about ourselves?

Sometimes happy mostly disappointed

THURSDAY   **Read Proverbs 12:18**

Journal in the space provided about a time when someone's reckless words hurt you. Pray for that person.

FRIDAY   **Read Proverbs 21:23**

List ways you can guard your tongue. What is calamity?

SATURDAY   **Read Proverbs 29:5**

What is flattery? Is it good or bad? Why?

SUNDAY   **Read James 3:3-8**

How can your tongue influence the way others think of you? What areas of your speech do you struggle with?

 LifePoint

The words we say have a lasting impact. When we speak without thinking or gossip about others, we are hurting—not helping—others.

ALL-GROUP
TIME:
Divide into
ler groups of
preferably in
·cle. You will
ave a small-
up leader for
"Say What?"

 Say What? *(15 MINUTES)*

Random Question of the Week:
If you could meet one superhero (movie or cartoon), who would you meet and why?

Group Experience: Silent Simon Says
Your leader will lead you in a simple game of Simon Says . . . with no words!
Afterwards, you will participate in a few discussion questions.

2

RGE-GROUP
TIME:
Turn to face
front for this
aching time.
ɔw along and
notes in your
ʻudent Books.

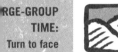 So What? *(25 MINUTES)*

The Power of Words

1. According to the old saying about "sticks and stones," what will never hurt us?
   Do you agree or disagree? Why?

2. Why would a person use words for the wrong reasons?

Learning from the Bible

earning from
the Bible ...

Proverbs
12:14,18;
13:3;
8:2,8,13,21;
21:23; 29:5

*A man will be satisfied with good by the words of his mouth, and the work of a man's
hands will reward him.*

Proverbs 12:14

*There is one who speaks rashly, like a piercing sword; but the tongue of the wise [brings]
healing.*

Proverbs 12:18

The one who guards his mouth protects his life; the one who opens his lips invites his own ruin.

Proverbs 13:3

A fool does not delight in understanding, but only wants to show off his opinions.

Proverbs 18:2

A gossip's words are like choice food that goes down to one's innermost being.

Proverbs 18:8

The one who gives an answer before he listens—this is foolishness and disgrace for him.

Proverbs 18:13

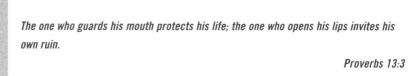

Life and death are in the power of the tongue, and those who love it will eat its fruit.

Proverbs 18:21

The one who guards his mouth and tongue keeps himself out of trouble.

Proverbs 21:23

A man who flatters his neighbor spreads a net for his feet.

Proverbs 29:5

LARGE-GROUP TIME:
Your leader will share some key points with you. Follow along and take notes in your Student Books.

Developing the Skill for Life – Using Words to Heal, Not Hurt

3. Give an example of how you can use words to develop and grow a relationship.

Words and their Effects

4. According to Solomon, words hold the key to what? What does that mean?

5. What results from reckless words?

6. What are some results of foolish words?

7. What are some positive outcomes of wise words?

Destructive Words
8. Where will destructive words never come from?

9. How can words be used to heal?

Speaking versus Listening
10. What characteristics cause foolish people to speak before listening?

The Friend-Separator
11. What could be an example of gossip?

The Flattering Salesman
12. What is flattery?

SMALL-GROUP
TIME:
Small-group
leaders will
direct your
discussions.
Everyone will
gain more if
you are open
and honest in
responding to
questions.

 # Do What? *(20 MINUTES)*

Making It Personal

1. As you look back on the past week, give one area of your life in which your words got you in trouble.

2. According to James 3:3-8, the tongue is like a small fire that quickly devours an entire forest. How would you describe the words you use with your friends?

3. Who is one person who needs to hear some encouragement from you this week? How can you encourage that person?

4. Have you ever been the victim of gossip? What did that experience teach you?

5. Complete this sentence with the ending that most appropriately describes how you feel: "For me to change the way I use my words, I'm going to have to…"
   - ☐ hear God speak to me in an audible voice.
   - ☐ know that others will change their words too.
   - ☐ find a new group of friends that understands the negative effect words can have.
   - ☐ talk to God and get Him to help me.
   - ☐ have a close friend keep me accountable for my words.
   - ☐ take a vow of silence!
   - ☐ Other: _____

The words we say have a lasting impact. When we speak without thinking or gossip about others, we are hurting – not helping – others.

These "Do" Points will help you begin to experience this week's LifePoint. Be open and honest as you answer the questions within your small group.

1. <u>Commit to pay attention to your words.</u> When you speak without thinking about the words you use, you get careless. Take the time this week to think about the words you use. Think before you respond to people. Even if someone sounds like they are crazy, you don't have to be the one to point it out. Just because others laugh doesn't mean it's OK. **Do you struggle with speaking before you think?**

2. <u>Notice people who need encouragement.</u> When you see someone who needs encouragement, take the time to talk to him or her with sincere words. Listen to him or her and respond with honest words. **How have you been affected by someone who encouraged you?**

3. <u>Be on the lookout for flattery and gossip.</u> Many times when people get caught up in the excitement of conversation, they share things they shouldn't. Commit to look for flattery and gossip and LOVINGLY (not angrily or rudely) remind people that flattery and gossip can destroy friendships and people. **How often do you think you hear flattery and gossip used? In what situations do you think flattery and gossip are most often used?**

Prayer Connection:

This is the time to encourage, support, and pray for each other in our journeys to trust God and seek out real and personal encounters with Him.

Share prayer needs with the group, especially those related to hearing from and responding to God. Your group facilitator will close your time in prayer.

Prayer Needs:

remember your
"Ready" daily
ble readings
questions at
beginning of
Session 3.

now What?

Deepen your understanding of who God is, and continue the journey you've begun today by choosing one of the following assignments to complete this week:

Option #1:

Go on a Flattery Safari. Be on the look-out for gossip or flattery. When you become aware of these moments, note them in a journal. Our discussion this week has suggested that we use our words to heal, build up, or encourage. Respond to every opportunity for gossip or flattery by using words of encouragement. Be prepared to let everyone know how many times you were able to turn the table on destructive words during your safari.

Option #2:

Meditate on and memorize Proverbs 12:18. Meditating means repeating the verse over and over while you think about its meaning and ways you can apply it to your life. You can aid memorization by writing the verse on an index card and putting it where you can see it to practice. It is best to work on the verse daily for at least a week.

Bible Reference notes

Use these notes to deepen your understanding as you study the Bible on your own:

roverbs 12:14   **words of his mouth.** That is, literally, the words he speaks (25:11). The good things we do and say bring rewards.

Proverbs 13:3   **guards his mouth.** Words produce consequences. James reinforced the wisdom of taming the tongue (James 3:5-9).

Proverbs 18:2   A fool has no interest in learning, only in airing his own opinions.

Proverbs 18:8   **choice food.** This is an apt description of a "juicy" piece of gossip. Just as a delicacy is digested, gossip becomes a part of us and affects our attitudes.

roverbs 18:21   **Life and death.** The tongue is the most powerful muscle in the body, but it also has incredible spiritual power in the lives of people. We can use use it to bring life or death to others and ourselves.

NOTES

LIVING SMART WITH PARENTS

 Get Ready

Read one of these short Bible passages each day and spend a few minutes wrapping your brain around it. Be sure to jot down any insights you discover.

MONDAY   **Read Proverbs 17:6; 30:11-12,17**

How important is your family to you? How do you treat your family?

TUESDAY   **Read Proverbs 30:11-12,17**

What is respect? How do you show respect to your family? Why do you think Solomon makes such strong statements about parents?

WEDNESDAY   **Read Proverbs 1:8-9**

Why is listening to parents important? What are the rewards of listening to a parent's advice?

God wants us to / its for
our own good.
a garland to grace /
a chain to adorn your neck

27

THURSDAY **Read Proverbs 4:1**

What kind of understanding have you gotten from your parents? Describe a time when your parents gave you instruction that really helped you.

How to be modest

FRIDAY **Read Proverbs 10:1; 15:20**

Do you have a responsibility to bring joy to your family? How can you bring joy to your family?

SATURDAY **Read Proverbs 23:24**

How does your family benefit when you gain wisdom?

SUNDAY **Read Luke 11:11-13**

What is the best gift you have ever received from a family member? What made that gift so special? How great is God's love and plan for your life as revealed in this passage?

 LifePoint

Learning to live life with godly wisdom makes family life easier. When we learn what our responsibility is in our family, life is better for everyone. God cares about your relationship with your family members.

ALL-GROUP
TIME:
Divide into
er groups of
referably in
le. You will
ve a small-
p leader for
Say What?"

 # Say What? *(15 MINUTES)*

Random Question(s) of the Week:
How is it that the villain always has kryptonite for Superman? Where do you get kryptonite anyway? Is it special order?

Group Experience: A Walk in The Dark
Your leader will describe a game called A Walk in the Dark.

After the exercise, respond to these follow-up questions:

1. How important was it to have helpers on your journey? How does your family help you on your life journey? When was the last time you thought about your family relationships?

2. As you think about your family, how difficult is it to honestly evaluate your relationships with them?

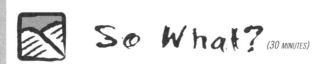

So What? *(30 MINUTES)*

Learning from the Bible ...

Proverbs 17:6; 30:11-12,17; 1:8; 4:1; 10:1; 15:20; 23:24

Learning from the Bible

Grandchildren are the crown of the elderly, and the pride of sons is their fathers.

Proverbs 17:6

There is a generation that curses its father and does not bless its mother.
There is a generation that is pure in its own eyes, yet is not washed from its filth.

Proverbs 30:11-12

As for the eye that ridicules a father and despises obedience to a mother,
may ravens of the valley pluck it out and young vultures eat it.

Proverbs 30:17

Listen, my son, to your father's instruction, and don't reject your mother's teaching...

Proverbs 1:8

Listen, [my] sons, to a father's discipline, and pay attention so that you may gain understanding ...

Proverbs 4:1

A wise son brings joy to his father, but a foolish son, heartache to his mother.

Proverbs 10:1

A wise son brings joy to his father, but a foolish one despises his mother.

Proverbs 15:20

The father of a righteous son will rejoice greatly, and one who fathers a wise son will delight in him.

Proverbs 23:24

LARGE-GROUP TIME:
Turn to face the front for this teaching time. Follow along and take notes in your *Student Books*.

God's Design
1. Who created the family? How was it created?

2. What three purposes did God create the family for?

3. What are traits of a healthy family?

4. What is communication and why is it important to a family?

3

A Big Responsibility
5. What are three responsibilities you have as a family member?

Show Respect
6. How can you show your parents respect?

Parental Wisdom
7. Give one reason you should obey your parents?

8. How can you learn from your parents' advice?

Give Joy
9. How can you bring joy to your parents?

The Road Ahead

1. What is the hardest thing for you to overcome in your relationship with your parents?

2. How difficult is it for you to imagine your parents were once your age? How does it feel to imagine that your parents once walked in your shoes?

3. How would you describe the perfect parent? Check all that apply.
   - ☐ Gentle
   - ☐ High expectations
   - ☐ Driven
   - ☐ Easy going
   - ☐ Loving
   - ☐ Helpful
   - ☐ Demanding
   - ☐ Easily won

4. Complete this sentence: "In order for my relationship to get better with my parents, I have to…"

LIFEPOINT REVIEW

Learning to live life with godly wisdom makes family life easier. When we learn what our responsibility is in our family, life is better for everyone. God cares about your relationship with your family members.

"DO" POINTS

These "Do" Points will help you grab hold of this week's LifePoint. Be honest with yourself and others as you answer the questions within your small group.

1. <u>Spend time searching God's Word for wisdom as it relates to family.</u> Take the time to read more from Scripture about God's plan for the family. **What can you learn from the Bible that will aid you in your family relationships?**

2. <u>Find a time for your family to come together weekly to talk.</u> Talk about your day at school and ask your parents about their days. Listen when they talk. Talk about things that made you laugh, things that made you sad, and things that angered you. Learn to communicate with each other. **When was the last time you spent time communicating with other members of your family?**

3. <u>Meditate on and memorize one of the verses from this lesson.</u> Meditating means repeating the verse over and over while you think about its meaning and ways to apply it to your life. You can aid in Scripture memorization by writing the verse on an index card and putting it where you can see it. It is best to work on the verse daily for at least a week. **Which verse do you want to memorize this week?**

3

Prayer Connection:

This is the time to encourage, support, and pray for each other in our journeys to trust God and seek out real and personal encounters with Him.

Share prayer requests you have with the group and make a note of any that others share. Your group facilitator will close your time in prayer.

Prayer Needs:

Remember your "Get Ready" daily Bible readings and questions at the beginning of Session 4.

 # now What?

Deepen your understanding of who God is and continue the journey you've begun today by choosing one of the following assignments to complete this week:

Option #1:

Take the time this week to meditate on the word "family." Read Ephesians 6:1-4. Look at your responsibility to your parents in this passage. Ask yourself the following questions:

- · What is my role as a son or daughter?
- · How well do I obey my parents?
- · How important is my family to me?

Write a paragraph explaining what you have learned about family and your role in it. Be prepared to share your paragraph next week.

Option #2:

Plan a family meal at your house. You can simply have your family show up at an appointed time, or you can have them join you as you prepare a meal. The quality the food isn't what is important here, what you do with the time you have together is. Discuss as a family your favorite memories together. Share what you have learned from this Bible study about your role in the family. After the meal, give each of your family members a note that tells them how much they mean to you.

Bible Reference notes

Use these notes to deepen your understanding as you study the Bible on your own:

Proverbs 14:1   ***builds her house.*** The focus here is on "house," which refers to a home. Providing a solid foundation for her family is one of a wise woman's great achievements.

Proverbs 18:22   ***finds a good thing.*** A good wife is a treasure and gift from God. We need to appreciate the wife or husband that God has put into our life.

Proverbs 19:26   ***assaults.*** In this culture the care of elderly parents was the responsibility of sons and daughters.

Proverbs 23:16   ***innermost being.*** This literally means "kidneys" and refers to who we really are at the core of our being, the real, deepest person that we are.

Proverbs 27:8   ***man wandering.*** When a man leaves home, he leaves not only responsibility but also protection behind.

4

BE COOL

 Get Ready

Read one of these short Bible passages each day and spend a few minutes wrapping your brain around it. Be sure to jot down any insights you discover.

9

MONDAY

Read Proverbs 10:12; 17:9
How can love cover all things? What things do other people do that make you mad? How do you cover them with love?

TUESDAY

Read Proverbs 15:1
What is your typical response when someone insults you? How did Jesus respond when people insulted Him?

WEDNESDAY

Read Proverbs 16:32
What makes someone patient? Is patience considered honorable today? Why or why not? Who do you know that is a patient person?

THURSDAY	**Read Proverbs 17:1**

Have you ever experienced a strife-filled home? If so, describe how you felt in that house.

FRIDAY	**Read Proverbs 17:14**

What happens when a dam is breached? Have you ever been guilty of starting an argument that could have been avoided? How did you handle the situation? What was the outcome?

SATURDAY	**Read Proverbs 19:11**

In what area of your life do you have the most patience? Is there anyone in your life that you have more patience with than others? Why does that person get more patience from you than others do?

SUNDAY	**Read James 1:19-20**

Think about James' command to be slow to speak and quick to listen. What would happen if you consistently followed James' advice? How would your family life be different? How would your relationships with others be affected? What would be the negative results of acting this way?

 LifePoint

As we begin to understand the destructive effects of anger, we must learn practical ways to reduce conflict and control our tempers. The skill of living life with patience helps control anger.

ALL-GROUP
TIME:
Divide into
er groups of
preferably in
cle. You will
ave a small-
p leader for
"Say What?"

Say What? *(15 MINUTES)*

Random Question of the Week:

If vegetable oil is made from vegetables and corn oil is made from corn, what is canola oil made of?

Group Experience: Someone in My Hand

You will play a game of "I Have Someone in My Hand."

q

RGE-GROUP
TIME:
Turn to face
front for this
aching time.
w along and
notes in your
udent Books.

So What? *(30 MINUTES)*

Learning from the Bible

earning from
the Bible ...

Proverbs
10:12; 15:1;
:32; 17:1,9,
14; 19:11

Hatred stirs up conflicts, but love covers all offenses.

Proverbs 10:12

A gentle answer turns away anger, but a harsh word stirs up wrath.

Proverbs 15:1

Patience is better than power, and controlling one's temper, than capturing a city.

Proverbs 16:32

Better a dry crust with peace than a house full of feasting with strife.

Proverbs 17:1

Whoever conceals an offense promotes love, but whoever gossips about it separates friends.

Proverbs 17:9

To start a conflict is to release a flood; stop the dispute before it breaks out.

Proverbs 17:14

A person's insight gives him patience, and his virtue is to overlook an offense.

proverbs 19:11

LARGE-GROUP TIME:
Your leader will share some key points with you. Follow along and take notes in your *Student Books.*

Taking Control

1. What evidence is there that we actually can control our anger?

Types of Anger

2. What are the different kinds of anger?

Anger and Love

3. How does love regard the other person?

Love Conceals Offenses

4. According to Proverbs 10:12 and 17:9, what does love do with offenses?

5. How does the enemy work through insults and anger?

Patience, An Undesired Virtue

6. How is a patient person a war hero?

Stopping a Conflict

7. What is the best time to stop a fight?

SMALL-GROUP TIME: Small-group leaders will direct your discussions. Everyone will gain more if you are open and honest in responding to questions.

 **Do What?** *(15 MINUTES)*

1. What is the most embarrassing thing you have done when you were angry?

2. Why was it embarrassing?

2. Check which response is easier for you:
- ☐ To walk away from a conflict
- ☐ To dive-in with insults
- ☐ To remain quiet and uninvolved
- ☐ To help resolve the problem
- ☐ Other:

As we begin to understand the destructive effects of anger, we must learn practical ways to reduce conflict and control our tempers. The skill of living life with patience helps control anger.

"DO" POINTS

These "Do" Points will help you realize this week's LifePoint. It's okay to be open and honest about your doubts as you answer the questions within your small group.

1. <u>Decide to give God your anger.</u> The way to make a difference in your struggle with anger is to actually do something about it and give it to God. **Are you seeking God in the areas of your life affected by your anger? Do you really want to let go of these areas of anger in your life?**

2. <u>Commit to learn to diffuse anger in your relationships.</u> When you get angry with people, you can affect their lives by showing them how you avoid letting anger rule your life. You can help others learn the skill of living life with patience. **What are two things you can do to diffuse the anger in your relationships?**

Prayer Connection:

This is the time to encourage, support, and pray for each other in our journeys to trust God and seek out real and personal encounters with Him.

Take time now to encourage and support each other by sharing your prayer concerns and writing down the requests of others in your group. Your facilitator will close your time in prayer.

Prayer Needs:

member your
Ready" daily
ble readings
questions at
beginning of
Session 5.

 # now What?

Deepen your understanding of who God is and continue the journey you've begun today by choosing one of the following assignments to complete this week:

Option #1:

Make a list of the actions of others that cause you to be angry. When someone commits an offense that angers you, make a note of it. Take the time during the week to pray over your list. As you continue to pray over your list and add to it, be sure to make notes of times when you avoid anger and conflict.

Option #2:

If you are artistic, take time this week to create a drawing or painting of something in your life that causes you anger. Talk to God about your anger as you are creating your artwork. When you are finished with your artwork, write Proverbs 19:11 somewhere on it. You can write on the back of your art or on the front. Take the time to pray about your anger and be prepared next week to share your art with your group. If you feel comfortable, give your piece of art to someone in your small group as a symbol of releasing your anger over that issue. Have that person pray with you as you release this aspect of your anger.

Bible Reference Notes

Use these notes to deepen your understanding as you study the Bible on your own:

Proverbs 15:1 Much like James, Proverbs makes the point that the way we use speech tells a lot about what kind of people we are (James 3:5-8). Whether we use gentle or harsh words, our conversation reflects our character.

Proverbs 17:1 *feasting.* This refers to feasting provided for by a family's peace offering. See Leviticus 7:12-17.

Proverbs 17:9 *conceals.* To conceal a sin is to literally overwhelm it with forgiveness and love.

NOTES

NOTES

PRIDE ROCK: THE HUMBLE SOLUTION

 Get Ready

Read one of these short Bible passages each day and spend a few minutes wrapping your brain around it. Be sure to jot down any insights you discover.

MONDAY   **Read Proverbs 11:2; 16:18**
Do you ever struggle with pride? When are you most likely to deal with it? What causes you to be proud?

TUESDAY   **Read Proverbs 18:12; 25:6-7**
What does the word *humble* mean? How is a humble person treated today? What is special about a humble person?

WEDNESDAY   **Read Proverbs 27:1**
How can boasting about the future make you guilty of pride? What is going to happen to you tomorrow? What will happen to you in the future?

Read Proverbs 27:2, 21

Is it wrong to receive praise from others? How can you get others to give you praise? When do you give praise to others?

Read Proverbs 12:9; 16:19

Have you ever twisted the truth to make yourself look better to others? Explain. Why did you desire to make yourself look better?

Read Proverbs 22:4; James 4:6

When you talk to God, how do you approach Him? Do you think God owes you something? Why or why not? Why do you think God rewards humility?

Philippians 2:8

What is humbling about Jesus' experience? Why did Jesus become human? What is the motivation for Jesus' humility?

 LifePoint

Pride causes destruction in our lives. Pride is sneaky. It creeps into our lives and is often difficult to recognize. Humility is the best weapon we can use to combat pride in our lives.

ALL-GROUP
TIME:
Divide into
er groups of
referably in
le. You will
ve a small-
p leader for
Say What?"

Say What? *(15 MINUTES)*

Random Question of the Week:
Why do we drive on a parkway and park on a driveway?

Group Experience: Who is the Beast?
You will watch a scene from the movie **Beauty and the Beast** and answer some questions about it.

1. As the scene opens, Gaston appears to be in the dumps for some reason. What does it require to get him back in good spirits?

5

2. How would you describe Gaston?
   - ☐ He's my hero!
   - ☐ If I saw him coming my direction, I'd turn around and go the other way
   - ☐ I want to be like him: big, powerful, and good-looking
   - ☐ He's a person I'd really like to be around: sensitive and caring
   - ☐ He's full of himself
   - ☐ He's the perfect man

3. When Gaston is in good spirits and having a good time, what does that mean for the rest of the group?

4. Is Gaston a person you'd enjoying being around? Why or why not?

5. In your opinion, what is Gaston's disgrace?

**LARGE-GROUP
TIME:**
Turn to face
the front for this
teaching time.
Follow along and
take notes in your
Student Books.

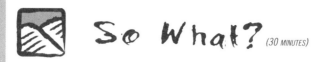

So What? *(30 MINUTES)*

Learning from the Bible

Learning from
the Bible ...

Proverbs 11:2;
12:9; 16:18-
19; 18:12;
22:4; 25:6-7;
27:1-2, 21

[1]When pride comes, disgrace follows, but with humility comes wisdom.

Proverbs 11:2

Better to be dishonored, yet have a servant, than to act important but have no food.

Proverbs 12:9

*Pride comes before destruction, and an arrogant spirit before a fall. Better to be lowly o
spirit with the humble than to divide plunder with the proud.*

Proverbs 16:18-19

Before his downfall a man's heart is proud, but before honor comes humility.

Proverbs 18:12

The result of humility is fear of the LORD along with wealth, honor, and life.

Proverbs 22:4

*Don't brag about yourself before the king, and don't stand in the place of the great; for
it is better for him to say to you, "Come up here!" than to demote you in plain view of a
noble.*

Proverbs 25:6-7

Don't boast about tomorrow, for you don't know what a day might bring.

Proverbs 27:1

Let another praise you, and not your own mouth--a stranger, and not your own lips.

Proverbs 27:2

Silver is tested in a crucible, gold in a smelter, and a man, by the praise he receives.

Proverbs 27:21

RGE-GROUP
TIME:
r leader will
re some key
nts with you.
w along and
notes in your
udent Books.

Beware the Lion Cub

1. What is real humility?

2. What are some examples of false humility?

3. What are the benefits of humility for us? For others?

4. What are some other words for pride?

5. Why do we love humility so much?

The Way to Disgrace

6. What is presumption?

7. Why does pride lead to a downfall?

Do What? *(15 MINUTES)*

1. How has pride affected you personally? How has it damaged your relationships?

2. How do you feel when someone is prideful? Do you enjoy being around them?

3. How is pride a part of your life? Check all that apply.

☐ I don't struggle with pride; ask anyone, they'll tell you how humble I am.

☐ I tend to focus on what I deserve in relationships and situations.

☐ I have a hard time focusing on others. I'm more worried about "ME".

☐ I try hard to focus on others, but pride keeps creeping back in my life when I'm not looking.

☐ Other:

Pride causes destruction in our lives. Pride is sneaky. It creeps into our lives and is often difficult to recognize. Humility is the best weapon we can use to combat pride in our lives.

These "Do" Points will give you a handle on this week's LifePoint. Be open and honest as you answer the questions within your small group.

1. Commit to spend time talking to God about others. The best way to combat pride is with humility. Humility comes from thinking about others more than yourself and seeing others as worth your effort.
   How much time do you spend talking to God about others?

2. Search for areas of pride in your life. Pride comes in many shapes and sizes. It can creep in quietly when you aren't alert.
   What do you need to do in your life to be on the lookout for pride?

3. Develop the ability to be real. Focusing on the approval of others takes your focus off God and keeps you from being concerned about others. When you are fake, people don't get the chance to know the real you.
   How have you tried to "cover over" your faults, mistakes, and the real you?

Prayer Connection:

This is the time to encourage, support, and pray for each other in our journeys to discover who Jesus really is and how much He cares for each of us. Share prayer needs with the group, especially those related to knowing and connecting with Jesus. Your group facilitator will close your time in prayer.

Prayer Needs:

Remember your
"Get Ready" daily
Bible readings
and questions at
the beginning of
Session 6.

now What?

Deepen your understanding of who God is and continue the journey you've begun today by choosing one of the following assignments to complete this week:

Option #1:

Focus on others this week. Don't make a show of what you're doing. Spend time praying for people when they don't know it. Look for opportunities to help. Pick up a pencil that someone drops in the hallway. Hold the door for your friends as you go into class. Be creative. Find ways to take the focus off of getting what you deserve this week; instead, give your attention to the needs of others.

Option #2:

Make a list this week of times in your life when you sense pride. Each day, find a quiet time and review your list. Pray about the pride that you discover and thank God for helping you recognize the arrogance that's in your life. Look over the verses from Proverbs from this lesson and allow God to change you. Be prepared to share your list with your small group next week.

Bible Reference Notes

Use these notes to deepen your understanding as you study the Bible on your own:

Proverbs 11:2   ***humility.*** This refers to putting both God and others before yourself. See also Micah 6:8.

Proverbs 12:9   ***have a servant.*** It's better to be of humble circumstances working for yourself than acting big, yet having nothing to eat.

Proverbs 25:6   ***place of the great.*** We should never "toot our own horn" or honor ourselves. The circumstance here is a feast, in which we are instructed never to take the place of honor, assuming our own greatness.

Proverbs 27:21   ***crucible.*** Our response to praise is a test of our true character. Silver and gold are purified with heat. Our character is also tested in the heat of life.

5

NOTES

THE BEST
4-LETTER WORD

 Get Ready

*Read one of these short Bible passages each day and spend a few minutes
wrapping your brain around it. Be sure to jot down any insights you discover.*

MONDAY

Read Proverbs 14:21; 21:21

How are kindness and happiness linked? Why would a kind person be honored?
Who do you show kindness to – friends, strangers, or both?

TUESDAY

Read Proverbs 12:25

How have you benefited from a kind word? How do you encourage people with kind
words? When was the last time you used a kind word to encourage someone else?

WEDNESDAY

Read Proverbs 20:6

Has a friend ever promised to do something for you and failed to do it? How did
that make you feel? Have you ever failed to follow up on a promise to a friend?
Why?

THURSDAY   **Read Proverbs 14:31; 22:9; 28:27**

Why do people avoid others? Why is it difficult to help someone who is needy? Have you ever been in need of something (lunch money, gas money, field trip money, etc.)? How did you deal with your need? How did it make you feel?

FRIDAY   **Read Proverbs 17:17; 18:24**

List your three best friends. Why are they so important to you?
How loyal are you to them? Why are you loyal?

SATURDAY   **Read Proverbs 24:17-18; 25:21-22**

Do you have any enemies? How easy is it to love your enemies?
Why should you love them?

SUNDAY   **Read John 13:34-35**

Why is love so important? What can people tell about you by the way you love others?

 LifePoint

A kind and loving spirit is characteristic of a Christian's life. People see Christ in you through the love and kindness you show others.

LL-GROUP
TIME:
Divide into
er groups of
referably in
le. You will
ve a small-
p leader for
Say What?"

Say What? *(15 MINUTES)*

Random Question of the Week:
Why do we refer to a "pair" of pants when it's only one item?

Group Experience: Play It Forward
The object of the game is to collect as many stickers as possible. Your leader will give you instructions.

The rules are simple:
- · You must allow someone to do a kind deed for you
- · You must give someone a sticker for doing a kind deed
- · You may not perform a kind deed for someone who you just gave a sticker to

You've got five minutes. Once time has run out you will answer a few questions about what can be learned from this exercise.

G

GE-GROUP
TIME:
Turn to face
ront for this
ching time.
v along and
otes in your
dent Books.

arning from
the Bible ...

Proverbs
:25; 14:21,
31; 17:17;
8:24; 20:6;
1:21; 22:9;
24:17-18;
25:21-22;
28:27

So What? *(30 MINUTES)*

Learning from the Bible

Anxiety in a man's heart weighs it down, but a good word cheers it up.

Proverbs 12:25

The one who despises his neighbor sins, but whoever shows kindness to the poor will be happy.

Proverbs 14:21

The one who oppresses the poor insults their Maker, but one who is kind to the needy honors Him.

Proverbs 14:31

A friend loves at all times, and a brother is born for a difficult time.

Proverbs 17:17

A man with many friends may be harmed, but there is a friend who stays closer than a brother.

Proverbs 18:24

Many a man proclaims his own loyalty, but who can find a trustworthy man?

Proverbs 20:6

The one who pursues righteousness and faithful love will find life, righteousness, and honor.

Proverbs 21:21

A generous person will be blessed, for he shares his food with the poor.

Proverbs 22:9

Don't gloat when your enemy falls, and don't let your heart rejoice when he stumbles, or the LORD will see, be displeased, and turn His wrath away from him.

Proverbs 24:17-18

If your enemy is hungry, give him food to eat, and if he is thirsty, give him water to drink, for you will heap coals on his head, and the LORD will reward you.

Proverbs 25:21-22

The one who gives to the poor will not be in need, but one who turns his eyes away will receive many curses.

Proverbs 28:27

GE-GROUP
TIME:
leader will
e some key
ts with you.
along and
otes in your
dent Books.

Generosity and Loyalty

1. What are some examples of me-centered thinking that prevent me from showing kindness?

2. What is the relationship between humility and love?

3. What are some earthly and heavenly benefits to showing love and kindness?

4. What kind of love gets the most attention?

6

5. What other kinds of love are there?

The Love of a Friend

6. According to Solomon, how can we recognize a true friend?

7. According to Solomon, loyal love is _____ love.

Loving Strangers, Enemies, and People in Need

8. Why is it especially praiseworthy to love strangers, enemies, and the needy?

SMALL-GROUP
TIME:
Small-group
leaders will
direct your
discussions.
Everyone will
gain more if
you are open
and honest in
responding to
questions.

 # Do What? *(15 MINUTES)*

1. Would you say you have enough friends, not enough friends, or too many? Explain.

2. What makes being friends with someone easier? What makes loving others more difficult?

3. Why is it easier to love some people more than others? At what point do you quit trying to love someone else? Can people ever reach the point where they don't deserve our love?

4. How do you love people who are unlovable? Can you describe a time when you made a special attempt to love someone who did not act like they wanted to be loved?

5. How does loving others honor God?

LIFEPOINT REVIEW

A kind and loving spirit is characteristic of a Christian's life. People see Christ in you through the love and kindness you show others.

"DO" POINTS

These "Do" Points will help you grab hold of this week's LifePoint. Be open and honest as you answer the questions within your small group.

1. Learn to recognize me-centered thinking. You'll be surprised where it pops up. **Where are the me-centered areas of your life?**

2. <u>Choose to become a loyal person.</u> Loyalty is not something that is reserved just for Bible characters or TV shows; it is something we should all pursue.
Are you loyal to your friends and the people you love?

3. <u>Develop ways to show kindness to others.</u> God desires you to be a kind person. He wants to help you be kind to everyone, not just those who are easy to get along with.
How will you show kindness to someone that is difficult to get along with this week?

Prayer Connection:

This is the time to encourage, support, and pray for each other. Share prayer needs with the group, especially those related to forgiving those who have wronged you. Your group facilitator will close your time in prayer.

Prayer Needs:

Remember your "Get Ready" daily Bible readings and questions at the beginning of Session 7.

now What?

Deepen your understanding of who God is and continue the journey you've begun today by choosing one of the following assignments to complete this week:

Option #1:

Read Matthew 5:43-48 daily for the next week. Make a list of your easy-to-love friends. Write down one or two reasons why you love each person on your list. Also, make a list of the difficult-to-love people in your life. Beside their names, write down one or two reasons why you have a difficult time showing them love and kindness. Spend time praying this week for your entire list, the people you love as well as those you have trouble loving. Let God speak to your heart.

Option #2:

Spend some time with a friend this week. Tell him the things that you appreciate about him. Don't just focus on the fun things that you do together. Take the time to let her know WHY you appreciate her. When you let people know you think about them and are concerned about them, you strengthen the bridge of friendship.

Bible Reference notes

Use these notes to deepen your understanding as you study the Bible on your own:

Proverbs 14:21   *despises.* Holds in contempt, belittles, ridicules. God held the whole nation responsible for their poor neighbors.

Proverbs 14:31   God is a protector of the poor (22:22-23). Our actions toward the poor reflect our attitude toward God.

Proverbs 24:17-18   *gloat.* An attitude of superiority. God detests this attitude—even when we gloat over adversaries.

Proverbs 25:21   *If your enemy.* Jesus taught this in Luke 6:27-31.

Proverbs 25:22   *heap coals.* When a fire went out, the homeowner would often borrow burning coals from a neighbor to start the fire again. In Egyptian culture carrying burning coals on one's head was a ritual of repentance. (See also Romans 12:20.)

7

·HONESTLY SPEAKING

 Get Ready

Read one of these short Bible passages each day and spend a few minutes wrapping your brain around it. Be sure to jot down any insights you discover.

MONDAY

Read Proverbs 19:1; 28:6

What is integrity? Why is it important in a Christian's life? Who is someone you know with integrity? How do they demonstrate it?

TUESDAY

Read Psalm 15:1-5

Which actions in this Psalm surprise you? How do you feel when you read a list like this? How would you rate yourself according to this list? How many people do you know who are qualified to live on "God's Holy Mountain?"

WEDNESDAY

Read Proverbs 20:17; 21:6

Have you ever been tempted to lie in order to succeed? Did you follow through on the temptation? What do these passages say about lying in order to gain fortune?

THURSDAY **Read Proverbs 11:20; 12:22**

How would you rate your own honesty? How important is honesty to God? Why? Spend some time talking to God honestly about your life today.

FRIDAY **Read Proverbs 13:6**

What is righteousness? What is wickedness? List some examples of each. Evaluate your own life. Which characteristic better describes you and your lifestyle? Explain.

SATURDAY **Read Proverbs 14:25; 19:28**

How important is it for someone to be an honest witness? Why do you think God feels so strongly against false witnesses?

SUNDAY **Read Psalm 26:1-3**

What do you think about David's prayer? Could you pray like this? In your own words, re-write David's prayer from your point of view.

 LifePoint

God takes honesty very seriously. We do not have the right to change the truth, bend the truth, or omit the truth for our own benefit. God honors honesty and despises lying.

LL-GROUP
TIME:
Divide into
r groups of
eferably in
le. You will
ve a small-
leader for
ay What?"

 # Say What? *(15 MINUTES)*

Random Question of the Week:
Why are the vowels in the words GOOD and FOOD pronounced differently?

Group Experience: Two Truths and a Lie
You will play a game of "Two Truths and a Lie."

After the exercise, ask these follow-up questions:

1. Which was more difficult, knowing who wrote the statements or which statement was a lie? Why?

2. How difficult was it for you to invent a lie? Did you try to create a "believable" lie? Why do you think people lie?

7

3. Describe a time in your life when you told a lie and got caught. How did you feel? Why did you choose to lie? What was your motivation?

LARGE-GROUP TIME:
Turn to face the front for this teaching time. Follow along and take notes in your *Student Books.*

Learning from the Bible ...

Proverbs 11:20; 12:22; 13:6; 14:25; 19:1, 28; 20:17; 21:6; 28:6

So What? *(30 MINUTES)*

Learning from the Bible

Those with twisted minds are detestable to the LORD, but those with blameless conduct are His delight.

Proverbs 11:20

Lying lips are detestable to the LORD, but faithful people are His delight.

Proverbs 12:22

Righteousness guards people of integrity, but wickedness undermines the sinner.

Proverbs 13:6

A truthful witness rescues lives, but one who utters lies is deceitful.

Proverbs 14:25

Better a poor man who walks in integrity than someone who has deceitful lips and is a fool.

Proverbs 19:1

A worthless witness mocks justice, and a wicked mouth swallows iniquity.

Proverbs 19:28

Food gained by fraud is sweet to a man, but afterwards his mouth is full of gravel.

Proverbs 20:17

Making a fortune through a lying tongue is a vanishing mist, a pursuit of death.

Proverbs 21:6

Better a poor man who lives with integrity than a rich man who distorts right and wrong.

Proverbs 28:6

GE-GROUP
TIME:
leader will
e some key
ts with you.
⌐ along and
ɔtes in your
dent Books.

Types of Dishonesty

1. What else does God detest besides dishonesty?

2. What is a common, yet dishonest practice about our promises
to pray?

3. List some types of dishonesty.

4. What two contrasts are made in Proverbs 11:20?

Lying

5. According to Proverbs 12:22, why are lies taken so personally?

Stealing

6. How does stolen food taste like gravel (Proverbs 20:17)?

Cheating

7. How is wealth obtained by fraud like a vanishing mist (Proverbs 21:6)?

Slandering

8. How can you be a false witness and not be in a courtroom (Proverbs 19:29)?

9. How does a truthful witness save lives (Proverbs 14:25)?

7

SMALL-GROUP
TIME:
Small-group
leaders will
direct your
discussions.
Everyone will
gain more if
you are open
and honest in
responding to
questions.

Do What? *(15 MINUTES)*

1. Where are you living right now in terms of honesty? Check one.
    - ☐ In the light. Honesty is very important to me.
    - ☐ In the shade. I admit I color the truth to suit myself, though I'm basically honest.
    - ☐ In the half-light. I have benefited from dishonesty, but I've turned my life around.
    - ☐ In the shifting shadows. I'm usually honest, but sometimes I can tell a HUGE lie – especially if it helps me get what I want and deserve!
    - ☐ In the dark! I need to quit cheating and lying right now.
    - ☐ Other: _____

2. Complete this sentence: "Dishonesty is a serious sin because . . ."

3. What thought inspires you the most to be honest? Check one.
    - ☐ Lying is a sin others find hard to forgive.
    - ☐ Cheaters and liars don't get away with it forever.
    - ☐ God delights in the blameless.
    - ☐ God detests lying lips.
    - ☐ God despises all dishonesty—big or small.
    - ☐ Other: _____

4. How can God help you become a more honest person?

5. How difficult is it for you to recognize dishonesty in others? How do you feel when you are dishonest with others? Do you feel like they know you are being dishonest? Why?

God takes honesty very seriously. We do not have the right to change the truth, bend the truth, or omit the truth for our own benefit. God honors honesty and despises lying.

These "Do" Points will help you grab hold of this week's LifePoint. Be open and honest as you answer the questions within your small group.

1. <u>Realize God takes honesty very seriously.</u> When we are dishonest with our words and our actions, a single person may not catch us, but God knows what we are doing at all times (Psalm 139). **Think of an example from the Bible that proves that God takes dishonesty seriously.**

2. <u>Focus on the truth.</u> Even though you might be tempted to present yourself as the hero in your stories, you don't have to. God knows the real you, and others have the right to know you too. Changing the truth to make yourself look better is wrong. **What keeps you from constantly telling the truth?**

3. <u>Recognize the advantages of being honest.</u> When you are honest, God is pleased, and He delights in you. Being honest brings blessings and helps you avoid discipline from God. **Do you know someone who is honest? What is his or her life like?**

7

Prayer Connection:

This is the time to encourage, support, and pray for each other in our journeys to trust God and seek out real and personal encounters with Him.

Share prayer needs with the group, especially those related to hearing from and responding to God. Your group facilitator will close your time in prayer.

Prayer Needs:

Remember your "Get Ready" daily Bible readings and questions at the beginning of Session 8.

 # now What?

Deepen your understanding of who God is and continue the journey you've begun today by choosing one of the following assignments to complete this week:

Option #1:
Pay attention to the words you say this week. When you are tempted to lie, take a moment to pause before you speak. Why are you choosing to lie? Are you trying to look good in front of your friends? Are you trying to get something you don't deserve? Are you trying to be included by a group of people? As you begin to recognize when you are tempted to lie, you will be able to avoid those situations. Before next week, write a paragraph detailing what you have found out about yourself when you are tempted to lie.

Option #2:
Meditate on and memorize Proverbs 11:20 this week. Take time daily to evaluate your honesty. As you look at your life, journal about a time when you lied and describe how you feel about that now.

Bible Reference Notes

Use these notes to deepen your understanding as you study the Bible on your own:

Proverbs 14:25

witness. A witness has the power to either save life or destroy it through deceitful testimony.

Proverbs 19:28

swallows. The practice of evil is a delight to the wicked.

Proverbs 20:17

gravel. This is an apt picture of the long-term consequences of sin. At first, getting away with something is sweet, but in the end we are left with the remains of our broken character.

7

NOTES

CORRECT ME IF I'M WRONG

Get Ready

Read one of these short Bible passages each day and spend a few minutes wrapping your brain around it. Be sure to jot down any insights you discover.

MONDAY

Read Proverbs 13:13

Why is it difficult to listen to instructions and respect commands? Who is the one person it is hardest for you to take commands or correction from? Why?

TUESDAY

Read Proverbs 13:18; 19:20

What life advice have you ignored? Why did you ignore it? What was the outcome? What advice or discipline has helped you most in your life? What advice or discipline has hurt you the most?

8

WEDNESDAY

Read Proverbs 12:1; 15:32

How are instruction and knowledge related? Whose advice do you cherish the most? What characteristics does this person possess that make you want to listen and follow them?

THURSDAY   **Read Proverbs 21:11**

What life lessons are you learning right now? What lesson have you learned because of discipline or punishment? Are you glad you learned it?

FRIDAY   **Read Proverbs 27:5-6; 28:23**

Have you ever been corrected by a friend? How did it make you feel? Were you initially angry with them? How did you overcome your anger? How is your relationship with that friend now?

SATURDAY   **Read Proverbs 27:17**

Who sharpens your life? If you don't have someone that is sharpening you, who could you approach about assuming that position in your life? What are the benefits of a sharpened life?

SUNDAY   **Read Proverbs 13:24; 29:17**

How do your parents discipline you? How will you discipline your children? Why is discipline important?

 LifePoint

Learning to accept correction is a sign of maturity in the life of a Christian. God uses many forms of correction to get our attention. Being corrected is not fun, but it is a vital part of our spiritual growth.

**ALL-GROUP
TIME:**
Divide into
ler groups of
preferably in
cle. You will
ave a small-
up leader for
"Say What?"

Say What? *(15 MINUTES)*

Random Question of the Week:
What was the best thing BEFORE sliced bread?

Group Experience: Rock, Paper, Scissors
You are going to play a game of "rock, paper, scissors" with a partner. Pay attention, though, because this version has a few twists.

When the game is over, answer the following questions:

1. How difficult was it to play a game when the rules were unknown? Why is it
   important to know the rules before you begin?

2. How difficult was it when the rules kept changing? What made the game more
   difficult, not knowing the rules or knowing the rules were always changing?

3. Who benefited from the rules? What is the advantage of everyone getting to
   make up his or her own rules? Why is it important to have one set of rules that
   everyone uses? Does conflict arise when you don't know what to expect?

8

So What? *(30 MINUTES)*

Truth in Criticism

1. What is one example of someone who needs correction?

2. Why do we resent correction?

3. Why does accepting correction seem particularly difficult?

Learning from the Bible

Whoever loves instruction loves knowledge, but one who hates correction is stupid.

Proverbs 12:1

The one who has contempt for instruction will pay the penalty, but the one who respects a command will be rewarded.

Proverbs 13:13

Poverty and disgrace (come to) those who ignore instruction, but the one who accepts rebuke will be honored.

Proverbs 13:18

The one who will not use the rod hates his son, but the one who loves him disciplines him diligently.

Proverbs 13:24

Anyone who ignores instruction despises himself, but whoever listens to correction acquires good sense.

Proverbs 15:32

Listen to counsel and receive instruction so that you may be wise in later life.

Proverbs 19:20

When a mocker is punished, the inexperienced become wiser; when one teaches a wise man, he acquires knowledge.

Proverbs 21:11

Better an open reprimand than concealed love. The wounds of a friend are trustworthy, but the kisses of an enemy are excessive.

Proverbs 27:5-6

Iron sharpens iron, and one man sharpens another.

Proverbs 27:17

One who rebukes a person will later find more favor than one who flatters with his tongue.

Proverbs 28:23

Discipline your son, and he will give you comfort; he will also give you delight.

Proverbs 29:17

**RGE-GROUP
TIME:**
r leader will
re some key
ts with you.
w along and
otes in your
dent Books.

Ignoring Correction is Foolish
4. What does Solomon warn will happen if we resist instruction?

8

Correction Is the Path to Learning
5. When it comes to correction, how are wise people different from foolish people?

Discipline and Correction from Parents
6. What is one role your parents are to play in your life?

7. Give two reasons why your parents discipline you.

Discipline and Correction from Friends and Family Members
8. Why should we listen to correction from family members or friends?

The Habit of Listening
9. What is a good habit that we can form to help us grow in wisdom?

Pruning
10. How is discipline like pruning?

11. List three ways our lives would be different if we welcomed correction.

**SMALL-GROUP
TIME:**
Small-group
leaders will
direct your
discussions.
Everyone will
gain more if
you are open
and honest in
responding to
questions.

 Do What? *(15 MINUTES)*

1. Tell the story of a time when someone corrected you in public and embarrassed you. How did it make you feel? Why?

2. Identify each example of correction below as wise or foolish.

wise *foolish*

☐ ☐ Honking and shouting to another driver to slow down and be careful

☐ ☐ Writing a note to a waitress explaining why she got a low tip

☐ ☐ Getting grounded for borrowing the car without permission

☐ ☐ Explaining to an employee that he eventually will be fired if he cannot smile and speak politely to customers

☐ ☐ Correcting a stranger who steps on your foot carelessly

☐ ☐ Telling an angry person to "calm down and get a grip"

3. How well do you receive correction? Check one.

☐ I'd rather visit the dentist and drill my own mouth.

☐ I enjoy correction because I like returning the criticism.

☐ I don't enjoy correction, and I often respond with anger or an insult.

☐ I can take it from a friend but not from a stranger.

☐ I can take it from a stranger but not from a friend.

☐ Other: _____

4. What would help you to receive correction more gracefully? Check one.

☐ Only brain surgery would help me!

☐ If I prayed for and studied God's wisdom on humility.

☐ If I learned to separate the anger from the truth of the criticism.

☐ If I learned to listen more and think less about what to say in return.

☐ Other: _____

8

Learning to accept correction is a sign of maturity in the life of a Christian. God uses many forms of correction to get our attention. Being corrected is not fun, but it is a vital part of our spiritual growth.

"DO" POINTS

These "Do" Points will help you grab hold of this week's LifePoint. Make an effort to connect with each other as you discuss the questions within your small group.

1. Make a list of frequent criticisms you hear about yourself. Write *True* or *False* beside each criticism. Explain how each criticism is true or false. For example, if you have heard that you don't make good use of your talent, you might put, "I need to be more focused and intentional" in the true column. In the false column you might write, "I am a passionate person who uses his gifts."
   Pray for God to guide you to grow in the areas in which people criticize you.

2. Spend time with a friend who sharpens you spiritually this week. When you want to get better at sports, music, or school, you take lessons. Imagine how much improvement your life could have if you found a spiritual tutor. Let your friend know you've been thinking about Proverbs 27:17 and your friendship.
   Discuss ways you've helped each other grow in the past and talk about ways you might be able to help each other in the future. Agree to be receptive to correction.

3. Meditate on and memorize Proverbs 12:1. Meditating means repeating the verse over and over and thinking about its meaning and applications.
   Write the verse on an index card and put it where you can see it. Work on the verse daily for at least a week.

Prayer Connection:

This is the time to encourage, support, and pray for each other in our journeys to grasp the importance of relationships to our spiritual growth.

Share prayer needs with the group, especially those related to finding and connecting with other Christ-followers who will help you to feel loved and accepted while learning more about God's plan for you. Your group facilitator will close your time in prayer.

Prayer Needs:

 now What?

Remember your "Get Ready" daily Bible readings and questions at the beginning of Session 9.

Deepen your understanding of who God is and continue the journey you've begun today by choosing one of the following assignments to complete this week:

8

Option #1:
Spend time this week listening to what others say to you. Are you often criticized? What are you criticized for the most? Are the criticisms valid? Truly listen, and write a paragraph detailing what you learn about yourself this week.

Option #2:
Write a letter to your parents telling them you are thankful for their correction. Share with them a time when they corrected you for which you are now thankful. Explain how you felt when you were first corrected and how you feel now. Tell them you know they corrected you because they really do love you. If you need to apologize for not accepting their correction and discipline, do so.

Bible Reference Notes

Use these notes to deepen your understanding as you study the Bible on your own:

Proverbs 13:24

the rod. In this culture the rod was used for spanking. Proverbs consistently reinforces the importance of discipline, regardless of the method of discipline or punishment (10:13; 22:15; 29:15).

Proverbs 15:32

instruction. God's discipline or moral correction is included in His love for us. Hebrews, as well as other New Testament books, repeats that truth (Heb. 12:7-11). We are to heed discipline or regret foolishness (5:11-12).

Proverbs 28:23

Rebukes are welcomed by the wise. But flattery is never effective with the wise and discerning.

IF MONEY TALKS...
WHAT IS IT SAYING?

 Get Ready

Read one of these short Bible passages each day and spend a few minutes wrapping your brain around it. Be sure to jot down any insights you discover.

MONDAY

Read Proverbs 11:24-26
How tightly do you hold on to what you have? Do you grudgingly let others borrow your things, or do you freely allow them to use your belongings? Why or why not?

TUESDAY

Read Proverbs 19:17
How does God reward kindness? Will you be more generous now that you know that God repays kindness? How can you be more generous this week?

9

WEDNESDAY

Read Proverbs 22:7
According to this passage, what is wrong with going into debt for things you really want? How does the Bible portray the person who is in debt to someone else?

THURSDAY **Read Proverbs 23:4-5**

Why is it so difficult to get rich? How can someone your age get trapped by greed? How does an obsession with money affect your life?

FRIDAY **Read Proverbs 27:23-27**

According to this passage, what do you need to worry about? How do you manage your money?

SATURDAY **Read Proverbs 28:8**

How would you feel if a close friend offered to assist your family, who was desperately in need of money. How would your feelings change if they charged interest in order to make money on the situation?

SUNDAY **Read Proverbs 28:27**

How do you define "poor"? Why is it so easy to look the other way when you see someone in need? Describe a time when you forced yourself to ignore someone in need.

 LifePoiNt

Money is a necessity in life; however, if you live your life solely for the pleasure money brings, you will be left feeling empty. Money cannot buy joy or satisfaction. God desires for us to use our money to bless others.

ALL-GROUP
TIME:
Divide into
er groups of
preferably in
cle. You will
ave a small-
p leader for
Say What?".

Say What? *(15 MINUTES)*

Random Question of the Week:
Why is the abbreviation for pounds (weight) lbs?

Group Experience: Blinded By Money

During this time you're going to participate in "Blinded By Money." First you'll divide into smaller groups. Then your leader is going to give each of you money.

You've got five minutes before regrouping to answer some follow-up questions.

RGE-GROUP
TIME:
Turn to face
front for this
aching time.
w along and
otes in your
dent Books.

earning from
the Bible ...
Proverbs
11:24-26;
9:17; 22:7;
4-5; 27:23-
27; 28:8, 27

So What? *(30 MINUTES)*

Learning from the Bible

One person gives freely, yet gains more; another withholds what is right, only to become poor. A generous person will be enriched, and the one who gives a drink of water will receive water. People will curse anyone who hoards grain, but a blessing will come to the one who sells it.

Proverbs 11:24-26

9

Kindness to the poor is a loan to the Lord, and He will give a reward to the lender.

Proverbs 19:17

The rich rule over the poor, and the borrower is a slave to the lender.

Proverbs 22:7

Don't wear yourself out to get rich; stop giving your attention to it. As soon as your eyes fly to it, it disappears, for it makes wings for itself and flies like an eagle to the sky.

Proverbs 23:4-5

Know well the condition of your flock, and pay attention to your herds, for wealth is not forever; not even a crown lasts for all time. When hay is removed and new growth appears and the grain from the hills is gathered in, lambs will provide your clothing, and goats, the price of a field; there will be enough goat's milk for your food--food for your household and nourishment for your servants.

Proverbs 27:23-27

Whoever increases his wealth through excessive interest collects it for one who is kind t the poor.

Proverbs 28:8

The one who gives to the poor will not be in need, but one who turns his eyes away will receive many curses.

Proverbs 28:27

LARGE-GROUP TIME:
Your leader will share some key points with you. Follow along and take notes in your *Student Books.*

The Love of Money
1. According to 1 Timothy 6:10, what is the root of all evil?

2. How is God's view of money balanced?

3. How will God's philosophy of money benefit you?

Pointless Riches
4. Why is it not worth it to wear yourself out getting rich?

The Generosity of the Wise
5. Why do generous people usually have plenty?

6. What is the key difference between a hoarder and a giver?

The Folly of Debt

7. Does the Bible forbid borrowing money? Why or why not?

The Folly of Selfish Enrichment

8. What is the definition of hoarding?

The Wisdom of Knowing Your Flocks

9. What steps can you take to know your "flock"?

ALL-GROUP
TIME:
Small-group
leaders will
direct your
discussions.
Today you
will focus on
connecting with
your heart and
connecting
with God.

 # Do What? *(15 MINUTES)*

1. Tell a story about the most foolish purchase you ever made. Why did you make it? Where is that item now?

2. How do you rate on the financial wisdom scale? Check one.
   ☐ Money disappears in my wallet.
   ☐ I'm so tight! I bring a calculator to calculate tips to the exact penny.
   ☐ I spend money so fast that I look like a card dealer at a casino.
   ☐ I give money away because it helps me get friends.
   ☐ I am looking forward to getting my first credit card. I already know what I'm going to buy with it.
   ☐ Other: _____

3. Do you believe God really cares about how you spend your money? What is something someone has done with their money that has really impressed you? Have you ever known someone who gives away money but always seems to have more?

4. Why do you think the Bible says God loves a "cheerful giver" (2 Corinthians 9:7)? How would you describe a cheerful giver? What motivates a cheerful giver?

Money is a necessity in life; however, if you live your life solely for the pleasure money brings, you will be left feeling empty. Money can not buy joy or satisfaction. God desires for us to use our money to bless others.

These "Do" Points will help you grab hold of this week's LifePoint. Be open and honest as you answer the questions within your small group.

1. <u>Commit to evaluate your purchases before you make them.</u> Are you guilty of buying things you don't need but want? Do you have a closet full of things you wanted last year but wouldn't be caught dead in this year? **How will you seek God's wisdom concerning your purchases?**

2. <u>Use money in a way that brings glory to God.</u> When we use money for God's glory to further His Kingdom, God is pleased. When we spend money without considering how it will affect our ability to give to God, we are not being financially wise. **How do you currently spend money? How can you become a better money manager?**

3. <u>Learn to be a joyful giver.</u> What is your attitude like when you give money to others? Do you resent giving what you have worked so hard for? Do you look for the money to come back to you? Do you feel like you're better than other people are because you gave (Mark 12:41-44)?
What is one thing you can do this week to be a joyful giver?

Prayer Connection:

This is the time to encourage, support, and pray for each other in our journeys to trust God and seek out real and personal encounters with Him.

Share prayer needs with the group, especially those related to hearing from and responding to God. Your group facilitator will close your time in prayer.

Prayer Needs:

ember your **eady" daily** **le readings** **questions at** **eginning of** **Session 10.**

now What?

Deepen your understanding of who God is, and continue the journey you've begun today by choosing one of the following assignments to complete this week:

Option #1:
Make a point to keep a budget this week. Yes, it's true, budgets are not very exciting or adventurous, but a budget is a great way to understand habits and tendencies. During the week, keep track of every penny you spend. This is a tedious assignment, but very do-able for a week. At the end of the week take a look at everything you spent and what it bought. Are you happy with your decisions? Are there instances that you wish you could "do over"? Be prepared to talk about your findings next week.

Option #2:
Find a worthy cause to donate money to this week. Do without something you want, or work some odd jobs for the extra funds. Look for a way to be wise in your generosity as you give without expecting anything in return. Journal honestly about your thoughts and feelings as you go through this process. Be prepared to share your thoughts at next week's meeting.

Bible Reference notes

Use these notes to deepen your understanding as you study the Bible on your own:

Proverbs 11:24   ***gives freely, yet gains.*** This is a paradox. Generosity, not hoarding, is the path to prosperity.

Proverbs 22:7   ***slave.*** Often in ancient culture people had to enslave themselves to pay off debts. The slave here refer to anyone in debt.

Proverbs 27:23-27   This passage celebrates the security and the cycle of an agricultural society.

NOTES

NOTES

THE LORD AND WISDOM

 Get Ready

Read one of these short Bible passages each day and spend a few minutes wrapping your brain around it. Be sure to jot down any insights you discover.

MONDAY   **Read Proverbs 10:29; 18:10**
Is God your strong tower? Why? What has He done to deserve that title?

TUESDAY   **Read Proverbs 15:11; 20:27**
How much does God really know about you? Describe something you have done when you forgot God was there.

WEDNESDAY   **Read Proverbs 16:9; 20:24**
How does God plan your steps? Can we choose to take a different path than the one God has laid before us? How could you have avoided some problems by following the steps God laid out for you?

THURSDAY   **Read Proverbs 16:33; 19:21**

What is something unexpected God has done for you? How do you know it was God? Have you ever used God as an excuse to do something you wanted to do so others wouldn't question your motives?

FRIDAY   **Read Proverbs 15:29; 16:5**

Do you think that what you do helps or hinders your prayers? Why?

SATURDAY   **Read Proverbs 19:23**

Describe a time when God protected you from evil. How did you feel about His protection at the time? How do you feel about it now?

SUNDAY   **Read Proverbs 29:25**

Why do we sometimes worry more about pleasing others than about pleasing God? Describe a time in your life when you tried to please someone other than God. What was the outcome?

 LifePoint

The road to wisdom ultimately leads to God. We become wise when we realize that God sees all, knows all, and influences everything that happens in this world. He punishes evil and favors righteousness. Wisdom is the Lord's, and those with wisdom fear Him.

ALL-GROUP
TIME:
Divide into
er groups of
preferably in
cle. You will
ave a small-
 up leader for
Say What?".

 Say What? *(15 MINUTES)*

Random Question of the Week:

Who is the funniest cartoon character?

Group Experience: Cookie Tower

You will work with a group to create a cookie tower.

After the exercise, answer these follow-up questions:

1. How difficult was it to see your tower fall? How did it feel to watch your tower fall because someone else wrongly placed a cookie? Were you disappointed to see something you created crumble before your eyes?

2. What is the one thing you are the most proud of "creating" in your life? What makes that thing so special? Did you take your time and put extra energy into creating it? Why?

3. What is the one thing you have created that has brought you the most disappointment? Did you have a vision of something beautiful in your head, but the finished project didn't come out that way? Describe what you created and how it looked when you were finished.

10

LARGE-GROUP TIME:
Turn to face the front for this teaching time. Follow along and take notes in your *Student Books.*

Learning from the Bible ...
Proverbs 10:29; 15:11, 29; 16:5, 9, 33; 18:10; 19:21, 23; 20:24, 27; 29:25

So What? *(30 MINUTES)*

Learning from the Bible

The way of the LORD is a stronghold for the honorable, but destruction awaits the malicious.

Proverbs 10:29

Sheol and Abaddon lie open before the LORD—how much more, human hearts.

Proverbs 15:11

The LORD is far from the wicked, but He hears the prayer of the righteous.

Proverbs 15:29

Everyone with a proud heart is detestable to the LORD; be assured, he will not go unpunished.

Proverbs 16:5

A man's heart plans his way, but the LORD determines his steps.

Proverbs 16:9

The lot is cast into the lap, but its every decision is from the LORD.

Proverbs 16:33

The name of the LORD is a strong tower; the righteous run to it and are protected.

Proverbs 18:10

Many plans are in a man's heart, but the LORD's decree will prevail.

Proverbs 19:21

The fear of the LORD leads to life; one will sleep at night without danger.

Proverbs 19:23

A man's steps are determined by the LORD, so how can anyone understand his own way.

Proverbs 20:24

A person's breath is the lamp of the LORD, searching the innermost parts.

Proverbs 20:27

The fear of man is a snare, but the one who trusts in the LORD is protected.

Proverbs 29:25

**GE-GROUP
TIME:**
leader will
e some key
s with you.
along and
tes in your
lent Books.

God's Wisdom

1. How is wisdom the creation of God?

2. How does the world's wisdom lack truth and value?

God in Our Hearts and Minds

3. Explain the significance between the Hebrew words for "spirit" and "breath."
   How is our spirit like our breath?

God Behind the Scenes

4. Why can't we predict how things will turn out?

God Directs the Madness

5. Why won't we ever be successful at controlling life?

God's Favor and Justice

6. Why do people doubt God's justice?

10

7. How does our obedience or disobedience affect how God answers prayer?

Under His Protection

8. How did a tower provide protection in ancient societies?

9. Compare your relationship with God to a strong tower.

SMALL-GROUP
TIME:
Small-group
leaders will
direct your
discussions.
Everyone will
gain more if
you are open
and honest in
responding to
questions.

Do What? (15 MINUTES)

1. How is God in charge of your life? What part of your life do you struggle giving to God?

2. How big a part does God play in your daily life? Check one.
   - ☐ I don't think about God during my daily life.
   - ☐ I feel God's presence when I am in church or small group.
   - ☐ I sense God in the quiet everyday moments.
   - ☐ I know God is there, but I'm not aware of Him most of the time.
   - ☐ Sometimes I sense God throughout the day, and other times I tend to forget Him.
   - ☐ God is always there, though I sometimes choose to ignore Him.
   - ☐ Other: _____

3. Do you believe God knows everything? How does that affect your life?

4. Do your friends think about God regularly? When was the last time you had a conversation about God with a friend? Where were you? Why did your conversation involve God?

The road to wisdom ultimately leads to God. We become wise when we realize that God sees all, knows all, and influences everything that happens in this world. He punishes evil and favors righteousness. Wisdom is the Lord's, and those with wisdom fear Him.

"O" POINTS

These "Do" Points will help you grab hold of this week's LifePoint. Be open and honest as you answer the questions within your small group.

1. <u>Commit to understand that God sees EVERY part of your life.</u> According to Psalm 139, we cannot get away from God and His presence. No matter where we go, God is there. When we understand that God created everything, we have nowhere to hide. **How often do you find yourself embarrassed by your choices when you realize that God is aware of what you are doing?**

2. <u>Eliminate areas of your life that distract you from God.</u> What would happen if you chose to stay away from a certain activity, event, place, or group of people? Would you be able to focus more on God?
Name two things in your life that are keeping you from God. How could you eliminate these distractions?

3. <u>Learn to accept the plans that God has for you.</u> How do you feel when random events happen to you? What is your first reaction? Do you view the unexpected events in your life as coincidence or an opportunity from God?
How can you release control of your life to God?

10

Prayer Connection:

This is the time to encourage, support, and pray for each other in our journeys to trust God and seek out real and personal encounters with Him.

Share prayer needs with the group, especially those related to hearing from and responding to God. Your group facilitator will close your time in prayer.

Prayer Needs:

ember your
eady" daily
le readings
questions at
beginning of
Session 11.

now What?

Deepen your understanding of who God is and continue the journey you've begun today by choosing one of the following assignments to complete this week:

Option #1:

God is all-knowing. It is true that He sees everything at once. As you go about your week, be very aware that the Holy Spirit is present. When watching television or talking with friends or even while you're out running errands, how different would it be if Jesus was physically alongside. How would it change your thoughts or how you perceive certain things? Come prepared next week to mention one instance and how His presence would have changed the circumstances.

Option #2:

Make a list of truths that you know because of God's Word. You might list items like "I know God created the earth" or "God is love." Think about the things on your list and imagine how your life would be different if you did not know these facts to be true. Pray for God to show you how necessary the Bible and faith are to gaining wisdom. Bring your list next week and be prepared to share it with those in your small group.

Bible Reference notes

Use these notes to deepen your understanding as you study the Bible on your own:

roverbs 15:11   ***Sheol and Abaddon.*** This is probably an allusion to the fact that God sees the dead in their graves or in their eternal homes. How much more should God be able to see the hearts of living people?

Proverbs 16:9   ***plans his way.*** God's sovereignty over our lives should not discourage us from planning and setting goals. However, we need God's wisdom to guide us.

roverbs 20:27   ***searching the innermost parts.*** King David asked God to search him out (Ps. 139:23). (See also Hebrews 4:12 for another way of being "found" by God.)

NOTES

·INTO FOCUS·

 ## Get Ready

Read one of these short Bible passages each day and spend a few minutes wrapping your brain around it. Be sure to jot down any insights you discover.

MONDAY

Read Proverbs 10:4; 12:24

At what do you work hard? Why? What are the rewards of your hard work? Is it possible for you to work hard at something that is not worthwhile? Why or why not?

TUESDAY

Read Proverbs 13:4; 14:23

Do you know someone who works hard at school? What are the results of his or her hard work? Do you know someone who wastes his or her time and talents regarding school? What are the results?

WEDNESDAY

Read Proverbs 10:5

What is procrastination? When are you most guilty of procrastination? Have you ever suffered because of it? Why do you choose to procrastinate?

11

THURSDAY   **Read Proverbs 14:4**

Do you ever think school is useless? Why? What things interest you enough to keep you involved? How could your attitude be better about school?

FRIDAY   **Read Proverbs 24:27**

Why do you think setting priorities is important? What are the priorities in your life?

SATURDAY   **Read Proverbs 12:27**

Do you take care of your belongings? Why or why not? Have you ever lost something that was important to you? What was your reaction? Could you have avoided losing it by taking better care of it?

SUNDAY   **Read Proverbs 20:1; 23:20-21**

How difficult is it for you to be self-controlled? Who do you know that has the most self-control? Who do you know without any self-control? Who is happier?

 LifePoint

Everyone can use a little more self-control and hard work in their lives. Laziness leads to boredom. God advises us to have self-control and to hard work in life.

ALL-GROUP
TIME:
Divide into
er groups of
preferably in
cle. You will
ave a small-
p leader for
Say What?".

Say What? *(15 MINUTES)*

Random Question of the Week:

How much time will an average American spend at traffic lights during his or her lifetime?

Group Experience: Banana Surgery

You will work with a partner to perform "Banana Surgery."

After the exercise, answer these questions:

1. Which was more fun, cutting the banana up or trying to put it back together? Why? What made putting the banana back together difficult?

2. If you would have known you had to put the banana back together, would you have done anything differently?

3. Did you feel like putting the banana back together was just too hard? Did you feel tempted to quit, or were you determined to make things work?

11

**LARGE-GROUP
TIME:**
Turn to face
the front for this
teaching time.
Follow along and
take notes in your
Student Books.

So What? *(30 MINUTES)*

God's Design

1. How did work figure into God's plan for humanity?

Learning from
the Bible ...

Proverbs 10:4,
5; 12:24, 27;
13:4; 14:4, 23;
20:1; 23:20-
21; 24:27

Learning from the Bible

Idle hands make one poor, but diligent hands bring riches.

Proverbs 10:4

The son who gathers during summer is prudent; the son who sleeps during harvest is disgraceful.

Proverbs 10:5

The diligent hand will rule, but laziness will lead to forced labor.

Proverbs 12:24

A lazy man doesn't roast his game, but to a diligent man, his wealth is precious.

Proverbs 12:27

The slacker craves, yet has nothing, but the diligent is fully satisfied.

Proverbs 13:4

Where there are no oxen, the feeding-trough is empty, but an abundant harvest comes through the strength of an ox.

Proverbs 14:4

There is profit in all hard work, but endless talk leads only to poverty.

Proverbs 14:23

Wine is a mocker, beer is a brawler, and whoever staggers because of them is not wise.

Proverbs 20:1

Don't associate with those who drink too much wine, or with those who gorge themselves on meat. For the drunkard and the glutton will become poor, and grogginess will clothe them in rags.

Proverbs 23:20-21

Complete your outdoor work, and prepare your field; afterwards, build your house.

Proverbs 24:27

GE-GROUP
TIME:
 leader will
 e some key
 ts with you.
 w along and
 otes in your
 dent Books.

God Honors Hard Work
2. Is work part of God's curse on this world? Explain.

3. What examples are given of God honoring hard and skillful work?

Work to Help Yourself and Others
4. Explain the relationship between hard work and success.

Work with a Purpose
5. What does it mean to gather in the summer?

6. What does Proverbs 14:4 mean about oxen and a harvest?

Work with a Plan
7. What does Proverbs 24:27 mean about first preparing the ground and then building the house?

A Hard-Work Attitude
8. Give some examples of how hard workers take care of their things.

Distracting Addictions
9. Describe how addiction is a cruel ruler.

11

SMALL-GROUP
TIME:
Small-group
leaders will
direct your
discussions.
Everyone will
gain more if
you are open
and honest in
responding to
questions.

Do What? *(15 MINUTES)*

1. What is the hardest job you've ever done? What made that job so difficult? How did you feel when you finished it?

2. How do you honestly feel about school? Check one.
   - ☐ I love it!
   - ☐ I like the friends I have at school.
   - ☐ I look for any excuse to miss.
   - ☐ I'd rather sleep all day than go.
   - ☐ I would enjoy it more if I got paid.
   - ☐ School isn't fun, but at least I'm learning something I can use later in life.
   - ☐ Other:_____

3. How motivated are you at school? Check one.
   - ☐ I'm more addicted to video games and entertainment than school.
   - ☐ I hit the snooze button four or five times before dragging myself out of bed.
   - ☐ After some caffeine, I'm ready to hit it hard.
   - ☐ I don't mind it, but I wish others would have a better attitude.
   - ☐ I would drop out if I could find a way to survive.
   - ☐ I'm satisfied and enjoy getting an education.
   - ☐ Other:_____

4. Which areas of your life do you need to commit to hard work? How hard do you work at your spiritual life? Why should you work on your spiritual life at all?

5. What can help someone who is addicted, whether it be to a substance or a behavior? Have you ever been affected by someone with an addiction? How has that affected your view of that substance or behavior?

Everyone can use a little more self-control and hard work in their lives. Laziness leads to boredom. God advises us to have self-control and work hard in life.

These "Do" Points will help you grab hold of this week's LifePoint. Risk being open and honest as you answer the questions within your small group.

1. Commit to work hard in all you do. Look for opportunities to learn and grow.
   What will you work hard on this week? How?

2. Search your life for distracting addictions. You might not be addicted to pornography, alcohol, or drugs, but you may spend more time watching television than you should. Honestly evaluate your habits and identify your addictions.
   To what are you addicted? How do these addiction distract you from hard work?

3. Recognize laziness in your life. There is nothing wrong with relaxing, but when you spend more time "relaxing" than working, you become lazy.
   Do your lazy times outweigh your active times? What can you do to become more active?

Prayer Connection:

This is the time to encourage, support, and pray for each other in our journeys to trust God and seek out real and personal encounters with Him.

Share prayer needs with the group, especially those related to hearing from and responding to God. Your group facilitator will close your time in prayer.

Prayer Needs:

Remember your
"Get Ready" daily
Bible readings
and questions at
the beginning of
Session 12.

 # now What?

Deepen your understanding of who God is and continue the journey you've begun today by choosing one of the following assignments to complete this week:

Option #1:

Pick an area of your life that you are not devoting enough attention to, and focus on it this week. For example, if it is school or chores, spend less time than normal on the computer, phone, or with friends to make up the time. As you focus on the neglected area, pray for God to give you the proper attitude about its importance. Journal about what you discover about yourself and the benefits or negatives of working hard.

Option #2:

Everyone has distractions that stand in the way of productivity. Prayerfully identify that "thing" that distracts you from being your best. It may be television or the computer, or it may be electronic games or idle time on the phone. Take this into consideration and begin a "Stop Doing" list. This may not mean cutting out something entirely, instead it may mean spending half of the time you currently use. Bring your "Stop Doing" list next week.

Bible Reference notes

Use these notes to deepen your understanding as you study the Bible on your own:

Proverbs 10:4 — *poor.* In Proverbs, poverty is usually associated with laziness or a lack of discipline.

Proverbs 10:5 — *harvest.* Solomon's culture was agricultural. He often uses the image of harvest to illustrate a person who understands the discipline of taking care of himself. In chapter 6 he used the hard-working ant to make the same comparison (6:6-8).

Proverbs 12:27 — *roast.* This may refer to the preparation of food or to preparation for the hunt. The point is that the lazy person doesn't adequately provide for himself and his family.

Proverbs 20:1 — *Wine ... beer.* Wine here refers to fermented grape juice. Beer was made from barley, dates, or pomegranates. Priests were forbidden to drink beer because it was so intoxicating.

Proverbs 24:27 — *afterwards, build your house.* Since the culture was agrarian, the first priority was establishing the land and planting the seed. After that the people could build houses and establish families.

THE EMOTIONAL ROLLER COASTER

 Get Ready

Read one of these short Bible passages each day and spend a few minutes wrapping your brain around it. Be sure to jot down any insights you discover.

MONDAY

Read Proverbs 14:10

What makes your heart bitter? What makes you excited? When was the last time you were genuinely excited? How did you act? Did you care who was watching your reaction?

TUESDAY

Read Proverbs 14:13

Have you ever put on a smile when you were sad? Why? How did you feel afterward?

WEDNESDAY

Read Proverbs 14:30

Would you rather be peaceful or stressful? Why? How does stress affect you? Do others notice when you are stressed? What do they say to you?

12

THURSDAY   **Read Proverbs 15:13**

How hard is it for people to know your emotions? Do you try to hide your emotions o
do you let others see how you truly feel?

FRIDAY   **Read Proverbs 15:30**

Who is the most cheerful person you know? Why is he or she so cheerful? How
important is it to you to share a laugh with your friends and family? What have you
done in the past that always makes you smile when you think about it?

SATURDAY   **Read Proverbs 18:14**

Which is worse, being physically sick or depressed? Have you ever been depressed?
What caused your depression?

SUNDAY   **Read Proverbs 25:20**

How can you best help someone who is hurting? What do you think this passage is
telling you?

 LifePoint

Our emotions are powerful. We can be paralyzed by fear and depression or ecstatic
because of a good memory or a joyful experience. In order to become truly wise, we
must learn to understand our emotions.

**ALL-GROUP
TIME:**
Divide into
ler groups of
preferably in
cle. You will
ave a small-
ıp leader for
"Say What?"

 **Say What?** *(15 MINUTES)*

Random Question of the Week:
Should vegetarians eat animal crackers?

Group Experience: Baby, If You Love Me ...

You will play a game called "If You Love Me, SMILE!"

When you have finished the activity, answer the following questions:

1. Which was more difficult, trying to keep a straight face or trying to make others laugh? Why? How did you try to keep your face from smiling? Did you have a hard time not expressing on the outside what you were feeling on the inside? Why?

2. What is the craziest thing you have ever done because you were "caught up in the moment"? What were the results?

3. What past event has made you the happiest? What has made you the saddest? Do your emotions ever get the best of you? Describe a time when you were emotional and didn't hide it.

12

So What? *(30 MINUTES)*

The Power of Emotions

1. How do different emotions affect us?

2. Why are emotions hard to see and understand?

Learning from the Bible

The heart knows its own bitterness, and no outsider shares in its joy.

Proverbs 14:10

Even in laughter a heart may be sad, and joy may end in grief.

Proverbs 14:13

A tranquil heart is life to the body, but jealousy is rottenness to the bones.

Proverbs 14:30

A joyful heart makes a face cheerful, but a sad heart produces a broken spirit.

Proverbs 15:13

Bright eyes cheer the heart; good news strengthens the bones.

Proverbs 15:30

A man's spirit can endure sickness, but who can survive a broken spirit.

Proverbs 18:14

Singing songs to a troubled heart is like taking off clothing on a cold day, or like pouring vinegar on soda.

Proverbs 25:20

RGE-GROUP
TIME:
r leader will
re some key
nts with you.
w along and
notes in your
udent Books.

An Emotional King
3. How did David express his emotions?

Emotions Are Personal and Real
4. Why is it a mistake to underrate emotion?

5. What are two sources of encouragement?

Hidden Emotion
6. Why do people hide emotions?

Influential Emotions
7. What is the difference between mere happiness and true joy?

8. How is understanding emotion related to wisdom?

12

SMALL-GROUP
TIME:
Small-group
leaders will
direct your
discussions.
Everyone will
gain more if you
are open and
honest with your
uncertainties
and responses
to questions.

Do What? *(15 MINUTES)*

1. Is it easier for life to bring you joy or depression? Why? Who affects your emotions more than anyone else?

2. When you are depressed, how do you react? Can others tell how you feel, or do you try to hide your depression? Do you long to be around others to cheer you up, or do you avoid others?

3. When you are joyful, how do you react? Can others tell your emotion, or do you try to hide your feelings? Do you enjoy the company of others? Do you desire to spend time alone? What is one thing you like to do when you are joyful?

4. Describe a time when you were either joyful or depressed and reacted emotion- ally. Did you care how others viewed you? What eventually changed your emotion

5. Complete this sentence, "When I am around my friends…" Check one.
   ☐ I try to let them know what my honest emotions are.
   ☐ I try to hide my true feelings because I want to fit in with everyone else.
   ☐ I wear a mask every day; I don't ever show my emotions.
   ☐ We don't worry about each other's emotions.
      We all have problems and agree to not talk about them.
   ☐ I don't care what they say about my emotions.
      If they can't accept me, I don't need them.
   ☐ Other:

Our emotions are powerful. We can be paralyzed by fear and depression or ecstatic because of a good memory or a joyful experience. In order to become truly wise, we must learn to understand our emotions.

These "Do" Points will help you grab hold of this week's LifePoint. Be open and honest as you answer the questions within your small group.

1. <u>Commit to be honest about your emotions.</u> When you hide your emotions, you silently tell others that honesty isn't acceptable.
   Have you ever hidden your emotions? Why? Do you have friends who can handle the truth about your emotions?

2. <u>Recognize the emotions of others.</u> Be on the lookout for others' feelings.
   Do you think the people in your life are being honest about their emotions? When you encounter someone who is joyful, how do you react?

3. <u>Encourage someone who is depressed or sad</u>. When someone is sad or depressed, the last thing they need is a false sense of hope. Telling someone, "Everything is going to be fine" can sound insincere and cliche.
   How can you offer encouragement to someone who is going through a difficult time? Which is more important to someone who is hurting, your words or your time and effort?

Prayer Connection:

This is the time to encourage, support, and pray for each other in our journeys to trust God and seek out real and personal encounters with Him.

Share prayer needs with the group, especially those related to hearing from and responding to God. Your group facilitator will close your time in prayer.

Prayer Needs:

12

Remember your
"Get Ready" daily
Bible readings
and questions at
the beginning of
Session 13 (the
last session in
this study).

 # now What?

Deepen your understanding of who God is and continue the journey you've begun today by choosing one of the following assignments to complete this week:

Option #1:

Keep an emotion journal for the week. When are you uneasy, sad, or lonely? When are you elated, peaceful, or content? Are you alone or with friends at the time? What seems to be related to your joy or sadness? Is it a circumstance, an experience, or a thought?

Option #2:

Become a journalist and pretend you're writing a story on the power of emotions. Interview friends, family, and teachers or coaches. Take notes. Learn from them how emotions have helped them in the their journeys, but also ways that emotions have perhaps gotten in the way or hurt. Ask about specific memories that still resonate in the deep places. Be mindful to remember certain words of wisdom that are shared. What kind of story would you write when your interviews are complete? Come prepared next week to "pitch" your story idea to the "editor."

Bible Reference notes

Use these notes to deepen your understanding as you study the Bible on your own:

Proverbs 14:33 *laughter.* Laughter is good medicine for our souls. However, while it may relieve stress of a person who is suffering, it is only a temporary escape from the reality of struggles.

Proverbs 15:13 *sad heart.* Maintaining sadness in our hearts crushes our spirits, creating discouragement, disillusion, and hopelessness.

Proverbs 15:30 *Bright eyes.* This is the sparkle or gleam in the eyes when good news comes.
strengthens the bones. This joy invigorates our body, mind, and spirit.

DON'T BE SILLY

 Get Ready

Read one of these short Bible passages each day, and spend a few minutes wrapping your brain around it. Write down anything God reveals to you.

MONDAY **Read Proverbs 18:2**
Do you listen or talk more? Why? Which is better, to listen to understand or talk to hear your own voice?

TUESDAY **Read Proverbs 18:6**
Have you ever spoken words that led to conflict? Describe one time and its outcome.

WEDNESDAY **Read Proverbs 13:14; 19:8**
What are some snares that you have avoided because of the advice of someone else? Did you listen to their advice immediately, or did you have to see evidence that they knew what they were talking about? Explain.

13

THURSDAY

Read Proverbs 21:16; 27:12

How can you stray away from wisdom? What are the effects of straying? How have you either escaped danger or suffered because you chose to listen to or ignore someone else's advice?

FRIDAY

Read Proverbs 10:19; 29:11,20

How important are your words? When was the last time your words got you in trouble? How did you reconcile with the person you offended? Was simply saying "I'm sorry" enough?

SATURDAY

Read Proverbs 11:12; 18:6

Have you ever been made fun of? How did you feel when others talked about you? Have you ever made fun of someone else? Why?

SUNDAY

Read Proverbs 24:3-4

Can you describe your life as a "well-built" house? How can your knowledge of wisdom found throughout this Proverbs study be a foundation for you to build on? What have you learned from this study that has affected you the most?

 LifePoint

No matter who we are, how smart we are, or how much money we have, we probably continue to make the same mistakes over and over again. We must pursue wisdom in order to keep our lives sharp and our eyes open.

LL-GROUP
TIME:
Divide into
er groups of
referably in
le. You will
ve a small-
p leader for
ay What?".

 # Say What? *(15 MINUTES)*

Random Question of the Week:
Why do doctors call what they do "practice"?

Group Experience: The Moving Quiz

The group leader will lead you in an interactive quiz. Be sharp!

GE-GROUP
TIME:
urn to face
ront for this
ching time.
v along and
otes in your
dent Books.

So What? *(30 MINUTES)*

Not as Easy as it Looks

arning from
he Bible ...

Proverbs
:19; 11:12;
3:14; 18:2,
5, 15; 19:8;
16; 24:3-4;
:12; 29:11,
20

1. How can wisdom seem deceptively easy?

2. What does it take to get wisdom not only in your head but also into your actions?

Learning from the Bible

When there are many words, sin is unavoidable, but the one who controls his lips is wise.
Proverbs 10:19

Whoever shows contempt for his neighbor lacks sense, but a man with understanding keeps silent.
Proverbs 11:12

A wise man's instruction is a fountain of life, turning people away from the snares of death.
Proverbs 13:14

13

A fool does not delight in understanding, but only wants to show off his opinions.

Proverbs 18:2

A fool's lips lead to strife, and his mouth provokes a beating.

Proverbs 18:6

The mind of the discerning acquires knowledge, and the ear of the wise seeks it.

Proverbs 18:15

The one who acquires good sense loves himself; one who safeguards understanding finds success.

Proverbs 19:8

The man who strays from the way of wisdom will come to rest in the assembly of the departed spirits.

Proverbs 21:16

A house is built by wisdom, and it is established by understanding; by knowledge the rooms are filled with every precious and beautiful treasure.

Proverbs 24:3-4

The sensible see danger and take cover; the foolish keep going and are punished.

Proverbs 27:12

A fool gives full vent to his anger, but a wise man holds it in check.

Proverbs 29:11

Do you see a man who speaks too soon? There is more hope for a fool than for him.

Proverbs 29:20

LARGE-GROUP TIME:
Your leader will share some key points with you. Follow along and take notes in your *Student Books.*

Wisdom Versus Foolishness
3. What are common consequences of living foolishly?

Wisdom Preserves Life
4. How is wisdom a "fountain of life"?

Foolishness Brings a Beating

5. How can foolishness be so devastating?

Wisdom Is Listening

6. In addition to reading from Proverbs, what is another godly source of wisdom, according to Solomon?

Foolishness is Speaking

7. If listening is crucial to having wisdom, how do the words you speak reflect that wisdom?

Wisdom Builds a House

8. Jesus talks about building the foundation on a rock. What rock do you think He is talking about?

 Do What? *(15 MINUTES)*

1. What is the most foolish action you have seen done in public? How did you feel when you saw it? Have you ever made a mistake like that?

13

2. What is the hardest part about being wise? Check one.

☐ My past mistakes keep creeping back into my life.

☐ I don't take the time to study Proverbs and learn how to be wise.

☐ My friends don't care about wisdom.

☐ I get busy, and I don't think about making wise choices.

☐ I'm still young; I've got plenty of time to learn how to be wise.

☐ I focus on making myself happy "NOW" rather than thinking about my future.

3. If you could gain wisdom in one specific area of your life, which area would it be? Why?

4. Do you believe God really cares about your choices? What choices does God leave up to you?

5. How can wisdom really change your life?

LIFEPOINT REVIEW

No matter who we are, how smart we are, or how much money we have, we probably continue to make the same mistakes over and over again. We must pursue wisdom in order to keep our lives sharp and our eyes open.

"DO" POINTS

These "Do" Points will help you grab hold of this week's LifePoint. Be open and honest as you answer the questions within your small group.

1. <u>Commit to search for wisdom.</u> The more wisdom you gain, the more your life will change. **How can you begin your search for wisdom? Where do you need to start?**

2. <u>List the important Proverbs and ideas that have helped you throughout this series.</u> Review what you have learned. Write notes about how you have been able to apply the wisdom you have gained. **What can wisdom do for you?**

3. <u>Focus on listening to someone whom you don't listen to enough.</u> Plan a time with this person just to listen and learn. When he is speaking, look him in the eye and focus. Ask questions. Try to understand what he is saying and why it is important to him. Afterwards, ask yourself, "Did I get to know him a little better just from trying harder to listen this one time?" **How can being a better listener give you more opportunities to gain wisdom?**

Prayer Connection:

This is the time to encourage, support, and pray for each other in our journeys to trust God and seek out real and personal encounters with Him.

Share prayer needs with the group, especially those related to hearing from and responding to God. Your group facilitator will close your time in prayer.

Prayer Needs:

13

now What?

Deepen your understanding of what wisdom truly means to us, and continue the journey you've begun today by choosing one of the following assignments to complete this week:

Option #1:

List the Proverbs and ideas that have helped you throughout this study. Review the verses you previously memorized. Write notes about ways you have been able to apply that wisdom to your life.

Option #2:

Meditate on and memorize Proverbs 18:15. Meditating means repeating the verse over and over again and thinking about its meaning and applications. Ask yourself questions like: *Am I in the habit of learning and observing? How can I live a better life today?* You can aid memorization by writing the verse on an index card and putting it where you can see it. Work on the verse daily for at least a week.

Bible Reference Notes

Use these notes to deepen your understanding as you study the Bible on your own:

Proverbs 11:12   **shows *contempt*.** This refers to despising or belittling.

Proverbs 13:14   ***instruction*.** This is any kind of teaching or training.
***fountain of life*.** This refers to the source of spiritual vitality and true fulfillment.

Proverbs 24:3-4   ***house*.** Any house, whether individual or family, is grounded in wisdom, strengthened by understanding, and prospered by knowledge.

Acknowledgments:

We sincerely appreciate the great team of people who worked to develop *Proverbs: Uncommon Sense, Youth Edition*. Special thanks are extended to Derek Leman for the content he composed for the adult study to which we are so indebted. Appreciation is also extended to Mike Wilson for writing the youth edition. We also thank the editorial and production team that consisted of Brian Daniel, Joe Moore of Powell Creative, Lori Mayes, and Sarah Hogg.

13

GROUP DIRECTORY

PASS THIS DIRECTORY AROUND, AND HAVE YOUR GROUP
MEMBERS FILL IN THEIR NAMES, PHONE, AND E-MAIL.

NAME	PHONE	E-MAIL